In the Dawn of a New Day

of a New Day

a gift of comfort

by Sam L. Hornbeak

In the Dawn of a New Day

by Sam L. Hornbeak

Published by:
Quail Mountain Publishers
P. O. Box 773
Dewey, Arizona 86327-0773

Edited by Kate Colby
Illustrations by Diane Yeager

ISBN 0-9633683-0-3

Library of Congress
Catalog Card Number: 92-64295

First Edition

Printed in the United States of America

This book is dedicated to the memory
of my mother,

Dorothy Hornbeak,

whose love, tenderness, and
unselfishness remain a strong force today
in providing inspiration for my writings
and for nearly every aspect
of my day-to-day living.

It is also dedicated to the memory
of my sister,

Betty Maxon,

whose graciousness and love were felt
by so many people around the world
through her career as the wife
of an Air Force officer.

The Dawning

How bright the morning after,
how fresh the new-born start,
as love now floods the dawning,
imparted heart to heart.

God's children live forever
in Life's unfailing light;
peel back death's masking error
and find there is no night.

Contents

Illustrations

About the Artist: Diane Yeager lives in Prescott Valley, Arizona. Her artwork has been exhibited throughout the state. In 1983 she was selected as a member of Womens' Artists of America West. She believes her talent is a God-given gift. This brings a spiritual touch to her work. She is a wife and the mother of two small children.

Preface

When I moved to the Pacific coast of California, I made an interesting discovery. While new to me, I'm sure it is taken for granted by other coastal dwellers who enjoy taking long walks on winter mornings. It had to do with the sea gulls nestling on the warm sands or grassy inland parks.

In flocks of perhaps a hundred or more, the birds stood close together, all facing toward the rising sun. Even when a dense overcast blocked all promise of sunlight, they still faced east-southeast. These swift-winged weather vanes did not point out wind direction or other physical phenomena. Instinctively knowing their source of warmth and light, they prophesied the dawning of a new day, never doubting its appearance, even on the darkest or stormiest of mornings.

9

Over many years, I have also turned toward the dawning of each new day with increasing expectancy. However, this expectancy goes much deeper than just the observance of a rising sun. It is a product of my growing understanding of the meaning and presence of ongoing Life. My faith in the eternality of life and the conviction that none of us can be abandoned by a loving Father has continued to dawn in my thought, having a profound effect on my daily experience.

This faith and conviction have enabled me to write the enclosed thoughts, poems, and letters, which have brought some measure of comfort and hope to family, friends, and the world at large.

My sincere desire is that this little book will help the reader emerge somewhat from any burden of grief and loneliness. Also, that it will help dispel remorse or guilt that may be felt for not having been more loving and attentive toward a loved one who has passed.

Our total family is the world at large. So much of this family cries out for a renewal of faith, joy and expectancy. Each of us can help to fulfill that need, but a sorrowful, guilt-ridden, or self-centered thought too often blinds our eyes and our hearts from discerning the opportunities at hand. I hope the words of this book will increase your own confidence in reaching out to comfort others in need.

Please feel free to copy any of the enclosed writings for your own personal use in comforting others. There are only two reservations: (1) No multiple or mass production of all or any portion of the enclosed, and (2) an acknowledgment of the author in any use of these materials.

May the contents of this small volume help you and others to replace tears with hope, loneliness with an awakened acknowledgment of the comforting presence of divine Love and ongoing Life, and faltering footsteps with a confident stride into the dawn of a new day.

Acknowledgments

No one has helped more in the publication of this book than my loving wife, Kate Colby. She encouraged me to make time for full-time writing, provided helpful suggestions, competent editing, typesetting, and assistance in every way with the final publication.

George and Marcie Young, who are successful book publishers, have been unstinting in their suggestions and help regarding the content, the publication, and the marketing of this book. I am especially grateful to them for taking the time to help a friend.

Other staunch supporters of my writing over the years include my sister, June Vogel, my brother, Jim Hornbeak, my children, John, Claudia, and Rita, and my many pen pals and supporters of my religious articles and poems. A special thanks also to Al Hicks, Claude Peters, Charles and Betsie Hutchinson, and especially to Danah Fayman, for their love and support.

I also wish to thank Earl Hatfield of Classic Printers for his patient technical guidance.

A grateful thank you to The Christian Science Publishing Society for permission to reprint some of my published poems in this book.

Section I

I'm Not Alone!

The heart that gives
is never alone;
to all mankind
its love is shown.

Loving Your Way
Out of Loneliness

To be faced with a sudden loss of family or a close friend too often results in a debilitating sense of despondency and the temptation to cut off all contact with the outside world. But isn't this just the opposite of what we should be doing?

There are so many people, including our remaining friends and family, who need our love and support. I am convinced that most of us have barely touched the surface of our God-given ability to love and care for our fellowman. We can stop pitying ourselves by reaching out to help others. Even someone who is a shut-in can find ways to share. Letters and telephone calls can so often light up an otherwise dreary day for a friend.

Let me share some examples from members of my own family:

My mother became a widow during the depression days at age 44 with three children still at home. She never ceased caring and sharing her love with family and friends for the remaining almost forty years of her life. Everyone loved mother because her own love knew no boundaries. In her later years she confided with me that she was never lonely. At that time, she had prayed and loved her way out of a severe case of arthritis which had confined her to a wheelchair for a number of years. In her early eighties, she remained active, even helping out a lady who was in her nineties! Mother had an assured sense of always walking hand-in-hand with an all-loving Father.

My sister also loved her way out of a sorrowful and challenging period in her life. Her husband died at age 36 following an operation for a cancerous brain tumor. With two children in school, she carried on a career, was remarried for a brief period, but has since remained single for many years. She lives modestly but is a wealthy woman if you add up the value of her many friends plus her family. I have watched her become a steadfast friend to her neighbors and fellow-workers each time she changed jobs or apartments. She feeds struggling students, bedridden older people, and helps to nurse them when a need arises. After retiring at age 70, she is an avid university student, travels, and still finds time to love and care for others.

My younger brother was a single parent to his young son and in addition became like a foster father to the family of a close friend who was incapacitated. I don't know of anyone who does not love and respect him. He even shares a daily ration of MacDonald's sausage biscuits with dogs belonging to friends. What a softy!

The important thing is that each member of this family has discovered an enlarged sense of family through loving and sharing with others. And so can you! Are you tempted to say at this point, "I've got all I can handle just to take care of myself?" Don't be. Why? Because the very best thing you can do for yourself is to turn from your own problems through reaching out and helping others. The light you shed will illumine your own day too!

Silent Prayer

Through heart-filled hush of silent prayer
God's healing touch dissolves despair.
Rainbows of hope shine through grief's tear. . .
I'm not alone. . .His Christ is here!

I'm Not Alone

I felt so alone. . .my love was gone. . .
how empty the night,
    how bleak the dawn;
but then came a whispering in my ear
"Just take My hand. I'm always near."

Who speaks so softly, gently, sweet?
If that's you, Father, please repeat.
"My angels enfold you, precious one;
they fill your heart. . .they're never gone."

But the human touch, the human voice;
to have that back is my first choice.
"Whatever you need, child, for today,
is right here for you, if first you pray."

"But, but". . . the wanting
    kept trying to drown
the gentle prodding of angel sound.
And then this message came loud & clear,
"Let go. Trust Me. I hold you dear."

Submitting to bended knee of thought,
Self-sorrow gave way
        to peace long sought;
I felt Love's touch, my heart grew full
as angels echoed this golden rule:

> *To the extent I listen*
> *To the extent I give*
> *Christ fills my life*
> *With the love I live.*

The Awakening

In the quietness of my tear-washed heart
the sense of loss, the grief, the holding on. . .
slowly. . .oh, so slowly,
loose their hold.

An angel's whispered message grows
more insistent. . .knocking. . .knocking
at the door. . .of my
grief-incarcerated thought,

"Wake up, dear one!
Life goes on. . .I created it. . .
ordained its foreverness;
it cannot be lost."

Gently, oh, so gently, thought beholds
the dawning of His promise. . .
the awakening
to ongoing life.

My tear-stained self-sorrow
now released uncovers
at long last. . .a smile
flood-lighting
grief-stricken night.

And now. . .the brightness. . .
the brightness of unending day
showing clearly the Father's delight
in all His children
tucked safely
in His loving arms.

I Can Do It!

Muffled in the cavern of my grief
I heard. . .what? A cry? A prayer?
Were others lonely as myself?

The outcry blended into
a prayer-filled chorus of
"Please, dear Father,
help us, remove from us
these icy stones of loneliness."

"Go, my son. Fill their cups
with the wine of your love."

The doubts, the clinging
to my own cold stones
melted in the imperative
of that command.

Then I knew. . .I CAN DO IT!
I can give of my love!
And I will!

Section II

Bridging Guilt's Abyss

Too late to go back
or make amends?
Not when we realize
Life never ends.

It's Never Too Late

Is it possible to span the seemingly impenetrable gap of death in order to make amends for negligence, anger-impelled splits in family ties, and unoffered expressions of love? I think it is. Not just in the hereafter, but here and now. Let's talk about it.

Have you ever seen the Royal Gorge in Colorado and its suspension bridge spanning a gorge whose base is over 1,000 feet below? It's awesome! Imagine how this abyss must have appeared to the early explorers of the region. I doubt if any of them would have envisioned a way to span that gap. There is very little that is deemed impossible in today's engineering and scientific communities. In spite of the great strides of science in overcoming physical limitations, we still seem too often to be in the dark ages in dealing with human emotions and in the understanding of our spiritual universe. How can we explore more deeply that spiritual realm, and thereby be healed of our burdens of guilt and regret? How can we span this spiritual gap?

Several years ago, one of my articles entitled, "Desert Dawn and the Hassayampa," was published in a church periodical. A lady in another state immediately wrote to share the following story about herself and her father.

In 1910 her father had worked in the Prescott, Arizona area. After he retired in the 40's, he wrote a poem about the Hassayampa River called "Song of the Hassayampa." One of the verses included the following:

"Drying and sinking, springing and slinking
pushing on where the Lord only knows
'cause no one cares or gives a darn
where the Hassayampa flows."

I understand that to the native Americans, Hassayampa means "disappearing river." Much of the Hassayampa flows underground except in times of heavy precipitation. In my article I used this illustration to make the point that even though the river appears to be gone, underneath the ground, its life-giving waters continue to flow. This hints at our spiritual life which I am convinced does not cease at the point called death.

Back to my friend. She and her sister decided to commemorate what would have been their father's 100'th birthday. They gathered pictures and his writings for the occasion. In her letter to me, she wrote, "Up to that time I hadn't felt particularly close to Daddy. I. . .was an independent little brat, I'm sure. . .There wasn't any open conflict and many good times but no great feeling of closeness. . .However, going through his writings. . .I gained a new appreciation of him. In fact, after spending an entire day reading, I was suddenly aware of a new warmth of feeling. Once awakened, it has grown steadily ever since."

So whatever regrets this dear lady had about not being closer to her father, have largely been resolved through her reaching out to him, even though he is no longer physically present. And I have a very strong feeling that the healing is flowing in both directions across this abyss we call death.

To me, my friend's story illustrates quite clearly that it's never too late to make amends, to rid oneself of regrets and guilt-burdens after a loved one has passed away. It may take quite a struggle, many mental footsteps, and a fresh outreaching expression of love to our fellowman to build a bridge that will span the abyss of death. When we reach the point where our love surfaces to tangibly bless our family, our neighbors, and all mankind, I feel certain that there will be a simultaneous shedding of these unneeded burdens. A heart that overflows with love allows no room for guilt and remorse.

Rebuilding Love's Bridge

How many times had I intended
　　to call. . .to visit. . .to write?
　　It wasn't that I didn't love her;
　　deep down, I always did.
　　Somehow, my busyness, my seeming inability
　　to say what was in my heart
　　encouraged the ever-recurring. . .
　　"Perhaps, later."

But now, she's gone. . .
　　or is she?
　　Did she. . .does she. . .
　　know of my love?
　　Did the love that was in my
　　senselessly-encrusted heart
　　somehow communicate itself?

Now that my tears have washed away
　　that encrustation,
　　is my overflowing love building a bridge
　　over this dark abyss of
　　doubt and self-accusation?

Each prayer, each reaching out
    with uninhibited love
    answers affirmatively.
    Little by little that murky abyss
    is filling in. . .
    filling in with increasing
    expectancy of ongoing Life.

Oh, my dearest one, hear my message:
    "I have always loved you
    even as I do now.
    The fingertips of my thought
    reach out to touch your heart. . .
    to ask your forgiveness. . .
    to enlighten your journey."

This emerging bridge of love,
    built upon prayer and my
    reaching out to others,
    is slowly spanning (erasing)
    guilt-ladened thought. . .
    and I am finally. . .

<u>at</u> <u>peace</u>.

Lessons from an Attic

They were both gone now
and in the basement
of my deep-settled guilt
I cried out. . .cried out
for a second chance
to heal the wounds
inflicted through
my own self-serving
and ingrown hurt.

Shaking off the hopeless
longings, as best I could,
I at long last climbed
the attic stairs out of my
self-incriminating past.

And there I discovered
my loved ones' gift. . .
that special love-encased gift
of their own repentant,
prayer-found assurance
of reconciliation.

It was not spelled out
in letter-form nor
underlined in verse,
but somehow I felt
their presence,
their touch,
and my dimly lit
attic-thought was
flooded with the light
of Infinity's forgiveness.

Not Guilty!

Innocent, I plead
as self-accusation
would make me accept
death's prevarication.

I can make amends;
Life continues to be.
Nothing can steal
innate innocency.

Section III

On Offering Comfort

Words which are spoken
from the heart
Life's healing message
must impart.

Without Reservation, Without Hesitation, Offer Your Love

Most of the world's religions embrace a commandment similar to that found in the Biblical book of Matthew, ". . .Thou shalt love thy neighbor as thyself." And most people try, at least in part, to be obedient to that commandment.

But ask yourself, how am I at loving my neighbor when he loses a member of his family? Do I feel so awkward, so inept, that I hesitate to even visit him? If I do see him, do I add to his darkest hour of sorrow by spouting out a lot of words that he is not ready to listen to? Or do I help by simply being there, sharing my love, assisting in small ways, and listening to what he has to say? If I am reaching out in silent prayer for ways to help him face up to his grief and start the process of recovery, the right words, the right actions will eventually unfold. Then he will find his own way to climb out of his pit of despondency.

Think about this basic truth: a caring, loving heart always communicates itself no matter how hesitant one may feel or how poorly-spoken the words. One simple sentence, when spoken from the heart, may be the key to reversing a deepening sense of self-sorrow.

Which of these is a healing message? "Oh, how awful, how sad we are for you. You have our deepest condolences." Or, "We love you. Now, how can we help?" No long, preachy message, no tear-filled bowing down in an already overflowing river of sorrow. Your dear friend needs your strength, your uplifted thought. Simply give of yourself, of your love. . .without hesitation. . .without reservation.

If you are drawing upon a reservoir of deep conviction of man's immortality, your simple words will carry even more weight and provide ongoing comfort for your friend. But wherever you are in your growth Spiritward, your heartfelt reaching out can help and heal. Just get out and do it! Your own special and unique way of giving is needed.

A Listening Heart

Stunned by the news,
I reached out in prayer:
    "Please, dear Father,
    help my searching heart
    to discern the unvoiced emotion. . .
    the unsurfaced turmoil. . .
    clothed in grief's garment."

The answer was there already,
but like a small child,
I needed to feel His strong hand:
    "Go on, my son, whatever
    you need in sharing my Love
    is already planted
    firmly in your heart."

After the hugs and tear-washed
voicings of love, I said, simply,
    "Tell me about it. . .
    tell me about my friend."

And then it all poured forth. . .
the sorrow, the regret, the guilt,
the "why. . .why. . .why now?"

Listening patiently, I at last
talked about the happy things,
the good things that could not die.
Smiles appeared, tears dried,
and a quiet peace found harbor
in our hearts.

It was a start. . .tentative. . .yes,
but still the first faint ray
of light in an otherwise
dark-shadowed day.

Now the years have passed
and the healing is complete.
Satisfaction and self-appreciation
have found their home in understanding;
expectancy is anchored in faith,
and love has reached out to touch

IMMORTALITY.

Go, Share Your Love

The call came early at six in the morning.
"Please come, father's passed."
There was no forewarning.

My neighbor, my friend, not possible I thought;
"Just what to say?" the challenge I fought.
My heart then responded, "Just go, express love.
They need your help, not timidity's glove."

I prayed as I went to that home I knew well;
asked for strength, inspiration,
to help break grief's shock-spell.

Then as I entered, self-concern dropped away;
my love they absorbed like fresh showers in May.
It was as if my dear friend had never departed
for his loved ones, like me
were in Spirit strong-hearted.

Never again will I entertain doubt;
expressing God's care is what Life's about.

Section IV

Follow Your Shepherd

The Shepherd of Life
will show the way
when prayer-filled thoughts
His words obey.

The Shepherd's Arms

Seeing myself in the Shepherd's arms,
    no lamb more closely tended,
I touch the hem of Christ's dear love,
    and grief's dark night is ended.

Adapted from a poem originally published in
The Christian Science Sentinel and Herald.
©1990 The Christian Science Publishing Society
    All rights reserved
    Used with permission

Comfort and Immortality

Comfort that gives some relief from sorrow or distress is a step forward. Hopefully, the words of this book and the verses in this section will offer such comfort. But the underlying tone of the book is that of encouraging the reader to push beyond temporary human comfort toward a conviction of his and his loved ones' immortality.

Moving from a sense of relief to faith and from faith to understanding, one becomes a minister-in-fact in the offering of comfort to his fellowman. He does not have to be a persuasive speaker, a poet or an accomplished writer. The healing factor is found in his day-to-day living. The effective comforter is one who expresses love toward all coming into the radiance of his deeply felt faith and spiritual understanding.

In recent years we have read and heard much about "near-death experiences." We would all like to believe that these instances give proof positive of man's immortality. The following experience took place many years ago with a member of my family and has helped to reinforce my expectancy of life beyond the experience of death:

My brother-in-law started working for a man at a very young age. His employer had no children so Andy was like a son to him. He helped the young man start his own business, but not too many years later, Andy died from an incurable disease. At the time of his passing, the older man was so ill that his wife never informed him of Andy's death. A month later, this man also died, but just at the moment of his passing, his last words were, "Hello, Andy!"

The more I advance in years, the less fear I have of dying, and the more certain I become that we will be reunited with those who have gone before us. But that reunion will not occur until we remove the self-applied blinders of grief, despondency, guilt, and disbelief in immortality.

For Christians, Jesus' resurrection and ascension provides the greatest hope and expectancy of their own resurrection. But the expectancy of immortality is not exclusive to the Christian religions. We must all follow our own hearts and innermost quest for this greatest of all promises. The Father I have come to know and love has room in His arms for all of his precious lambs.

New Horizons

In the first hint of light
at the break of day,
I discover my path
is the Shepherd's way.

Fresh confidence takes hold;
I reach for His hand
as bright rainbows of hope
new horizons expand.

No "Holden" Eye

(an Easter message
based on Luke 24: 13-32)

Cleopas's eyes were holden
      (his earthbound thought aggrieved
            by those who sought to stay
               Christ's power)
Blind to what Jesus achieved.

No holden eye discerns, this morn,
      the living proof now found;
            Mary's love still whispers
               "Rabboni!" joyous sound!

Powerless cross, empty tomb
      erase all Thomas-doubt;
            "He demonstrates eternal Life,"
            the very angels shout.

With humbled heart I listen
    to the Master's strong command
       "Go, and do thou likewise"
        (your Christliness expand).

Bright Easter morn, fresh dawning,
    firms now my faltering step;
       The Messiah opens holden eye,
        His promise forever kept.

Surrender Not

The ghostly sense of dying,
the suffocating thought
imbedded in self-sorrow
are not what Jesus taught.

Don't admit this is the end;
withdraw the darkened veil;
see your God -- see His Christ
and know that all is well.

Our Spiritual Universe

Of its glorious majesty
we stand in awe!

A Michelangelo
can only hint at its beauty.
Shakespeare at his best
could not have described
its dynamic existence.

But a lowly carpenter gave
sure evidence of its presence.

The awakening to its reality
shakes our very being, decries
our long repose.

Hearts touched and sandals shed,
we bow before its Maker;
reach out to touch
His Christ.

The Music of Life

No final curtain call on life,
        no heart-dulling diminuendo,
no grief to stop the ear attuned
        to its continuous glad crescendo.

Section V

Comfort for Family and Friends

My loved ones are permanent
residents of my heart. . .
They can never be outside my love
and never forsaken by the Father.

"For They Shall Be Comforted"

"Blessed are they that mourn:
for they shall be comforted."
. . .Matthew 5:4

This section is addressed to you who have known firsthand what it means to lose a loved member of your family or a friend who is as close to you as family. Since I see my family as universal, I wish I could be with you face-to-face, hold you in my arms, and let you know I care. You are dearly loved you know, not just by me, but by all who are impelled by our Father's love to comfort their fellowman.

Most of the poems and excerpts from letters herein were written for family and friends who had experienced the death of someone close to their hearts. I pray that they will in some measure support you as you work your way out of "the valley of the shadow of death."

My Father Stands Before Me

My father stands before me. . .
his eyes fixed on the light;
passing beyond death's valley,
he's ever in God's sight.

"My love has never left you."
His words sound in my heart;
"Don't mourn, my precious daughter,
my love I still impart.

"Tuck your mother in your arms;
express your love and mine.
Open now the precious book;
Life's message you will find.

"We're closer now than ever;
the Ascension makes it clear;
Christ never died. . .nor can I,
dearest child, you need not fear."

The following are excerpts from a letter written to a young friend upon the passing of her mother:

I want to join my wife in expressing our love to you at this time of proving. . .proving the absolute reality of the many Life-lessons you have learned over the years.

One of the most difficult tasks we have is to fully release those we dearly love as they continue on their way in working out their full salvation. Because of your own strong understanding of indestructible Life, I feel sure you will be able to release your dear mother as she continues on her way. And carrying on, she certainly is. It may not be easy to see her right now, but you have not lost one iota of your mother's love. . .yes, not even her presence in Truth.

A Mother's Message

Dear ones, I never left you;
my love and care remain
to nourish and support you
until we meet again.

Don't feel that I am lost now;
the Shepherd tucks me in.
Supported by His angels
God's strength is mine again.

Go forward now -- live your dreams!
Let memories renew
the knowledge that I'm with you
in all that you pursue.

I'm proud of all my children,
of all that you have done.
So try to see as I do
that life through Christ is won.

This Child

This child is yours forever;
you hold her in your heart.
Love's conception is complete
and death can have no part.

Feel her hand in yours, dear one;
hear angel voices sing,
telling of the peace she's found
which only God can bring.

Excerpts from a letter to a friend whose son was lost in a tragic happening at home:

It is never easy to see our loved ones pass on, especially under circumstances such as that with your son. I just wanted you to know that my love and sympathy are with you and your family.

It has always been comforting to me to see life in a much grander perspective than that which seems to be included in our all too brief human experience; also to know that a God of love would never permit his son to die or to continue in suffering.

I am sure your son would not want his parents and family to be bowed down in grief and sorrow at this time. He is continuing to work in God's garden in which there can only be progressive beauty, harmony, and immortality.

The challenge now is to see that this statement is far more than mere words of comfort. It is an actuality.

While we cherish the memory of our human experiences with those we love, we must still be unselfish enough to release them as they continue on their journey from material sense to infinite Spirit.

The greatest tribute you can pay your son is to strive diligently to erase that last terrible picture of death from your thought -- to acknowledge that he is continuing on his way to accomplishments that you and I can scarcely comprehend. Also, to see that he is safe and well in the Father's hands and that, in reality, he has not been snatched away from your care and love.

I know that you will be able to meet this great challenge to your faith and understanding and that both you and your son will emerge as victors.

In His Father's Care

Yes, cry for now, my dearest,
but never in despair;
every breeze will whisper,
"He's in his Father's care."

Cherish what we had, my love,
for lost it cannot be;
remember now Christ's teaching;
its truth will set you free.

A Message to my Loved One

Allow no sorrowful drawn-out wake
to steal your joy away;
our hearts unite when life is lived
in ever-dawning day.

So take God's hand -- feel His love;
walk in expectancy;
as you express Life's fullness
you're drawing close to me.

Refusal and Affirmation

I refuse to drown in sorrow
you would not want it so;
I affirm life's endless promise --
its completeness you now know.

I refuse to grieve, my dearest,
cessation cannot be;
I affirm God's resurrection
includes both you and me.

Excerpts from a letter to my enlarged family after the passing of a cousin:

You know, dearest cousins, I have gained such an absolute conviction that this thing we call death is never a final curtain call on life. Rather is it a whole new awakening -- a whole new beginning.

Our cousin realizes this now more than ever before, and she will be waiting with shining eyes and uninterrupted love to welcome us as we pass through this mislabeled happening called death. Life is too special, too beautiful, and too God-bestowed to be limited to this brief period of time allocated as mortal existence.

So for our dear one's sake and for all our parents, grandparents, and other loved ones who have gone on before us, let's celebrate LIFE -- unshakable, uninterrupted life, not with gloominess or sadness, but with joyous expectancy, with humor, with love, with going on to help and care for each other.

What a love-offering this will be to our dear cousin as she continues on her journey. She would not have it any other way. Right?

Where is your Life, Dear One?

Where is your life, dear one?
Right where its always been;
its in the Father's hands
where it will never end.

Where is that light of Life?
In heaven's shining glow
where angels sing His praise
and all God's love bestow.

The Shepherd's gentle arms
enfold me in delight.
The sounds of morning song
erase the fear of night.

So bid no sad farewells;
my love is with you still.
Pain can no more touch me;
pure peace of Mind I feel.

Where is your love, dear one?
With family and friends.
It never left -- it never will;
steadfastness never ends.

On Wings of Love

On wings of love I've flown away
to a higher plane, to a brighter day.
My heart's music is with you still;
rejoice with me in all things real.

Soul's light now shines in radiant hues;
transcendent Life is mine to choose.
The sweetest song I've ever heard
now sounds beyond the spoken word.

Lessons of Christ horizons spand;
through Scripture's light I understand.
Let tears not blur nor night obscure
the fact that Life, not death, is sure.

Section VI

Answering the Child-Heart

In simple terms
your child will know
the love and truth
your hearts bestow.

When your Child Asks

Have you ever been questioned about death and the hereafter by your child or grandchild? Most of us have.

I have always been very close to my grandson, Stevie. He started asking penetrating questions at a very young age. I answered him as best I could based on my own beliefs. You, the reader, would answer your young ones based upon your own beliefs. I can only hope that your answers will strengthen the child's expectation of salvation and continuing life.

The following fictional exchange is somewhat similar to my talks with Stevie. We owned a small ranchette in Texas at the time and Stevie loved to be with us on as many weekends as possible. It was a very special time for this grandfather, and judging by our continuing closeness (Stevie is now seventeen), it was special for Stevie also.

Porch-swing Explanations

"Where is Great Granny now Grandpa?" It had been Stevie's first encounter with the passing of a family member. He was deeply puzzled as he had come to love his kind and gentle great grandmother and he missed her.

Grandpa snuggled the boy up closer as they slowly moved back and forth on the porch swing. A gentle breeze swept the late spring grasses of the small ranchette. A coyote called plaintively to the huge new moon as it rose above the surrounding hills. His only reply was from a great horned owl perched atop a nearby telephone pole. This must have satisfied the coyote because it was several minutes before he called again. The stars were unusually bright on this crystal clear night.

It was a time which lent itself to the probing of life's deeper questions. A single tear formed in Grandpa's eye as he blew his nose on a red bandanna handerkerchief. "Well, Stevie, most everyone who knew your Great Granny would say that she is in heaven right now. And I'm sure she is too, depending on what and where you think heaven is."

"Tell me about heaven, Grandpa. Is it as nice as our ranch?"

"I'm sure that it is even nicer, Stevie. None of us know for sure what it's like. Some people think it's far away, farther than the farthest star you can see. I kinda' have a different feeling. Close your eyes a minute, son. Good! Now think about all the most wonderful and beautiful things you have ever known. The moon, the stars, the fields, the flowers, the fluffy white clouds, the smiles on peoples' faces, the hymns being sung in church, the fun laughs when you play with your friends, you and I sitting close together on this swing. Got it, Stevie?"

"Yes, Grandpa. Can I open my eyes now?"

"Sure, Stevie. Did you see all those things when your eyes were closed?" The boy nodded his assent. "Well, that's sort of the way I see heaven. Only an even more beautiful and happy place. And I see it all around us. Everything that is beautiful and good and fun, we can find just by thinking about it. Like what you saw when your eyes were closed. In fact, I think you and I are in heaven, right now, also. It's just that we don't stop very often to think about it."

"Then why can't I see Great Granny?"

"Close your eyes again, Stevie." The boy obliged.

"Now think about your Great Granny. What do you see?"

"Cookies. . .oatmeal cookies."

"Why cookies?"

"Because she always made cookies for me."

"Why did she do that, Stevie?"

"Cause she loved me."

"What is love, Stevie?"

"It's something that makes you feel good all over."

"Can you feel her love right now?"

"Yes. . .yes I do, Grandpa."

"Then her love has not gone away has it?"

"No, Grandpa."

"Let's remember that, Stevie. If you still feel her love and she is in heaven, then heaven must be as close to you as I am. Do you understand that?"

"Sure, Grandpa. Great Granny must be close to me 'cause I can still feel her love. You know what, Grandpa, I can almost smell her cookies in the oven! It must be wonderful being in heaven."

"It is, son. It is. It's where you and I and Great Granny are, right at this very minute!"

"Can I open my eyes, now?"

"You bet!"

"Grandpa?"

"Yes, Stevie?"

"Why do people die?"

"That's kinda' hard to answer, Stevie. But you know what? I think there are a lot of people that don't see what you just found out. They think that when people die, they are gone forever. But you and I know that Great Granny's love and all of the other good things about her are still here with us. All we have to do is close our eyes, think about her, and there she is. Course, we don't see her like we used to, but some day we will see her like she is right now when we join her all the way in heaven."

"Grandpa?"

"Yes, Stevie?"

"I love you, Grandpa."

"I love you too, Stevie."

Section VII

Comfort for Family and Friends
of those in Uniform

Courage is the sinew
of those heeding freedom's call;
their love for God and country
lives on in the hearts of all.

The Ultimate Sacrifice. . .
The Ultimate Reward

What kind of citizen is one who is willing to put his or her life on the line to protect the lives and freedoms of his fellowman? The answer is simple really. Not some superman or woman. But someone who cares enough about his fellowman to do the job. It could be the son or daughter of the family next door who becomes a soldier, fireman, or policeman. In wartime, it might be a father or mother with a family to worry about.

Sure, there are a relative few who take the job (and abuse the job) simply because of their love of violence and combat. But in my experience during combat in World War II, I didn't know a single airman who carried on with this motivation. Most of us dreaded our combat role and pushed to get it over with as soon as possible. It was not easy to accept killing and sacrifice on either side of the line of combat. Our prayers were not alone for our own protection, but for a quick resolution of the entire conflict.

The 91st Psalm, or the equivalent thereof in other tongues and religions, brought hope and comfort on both sides of the fighting front. I literally wore out that page in my Bible. Presently, in thinking about my comrades in arms who died in combat or have passed on since that time, my concentration is more on the last two paragraphs: ". . .I will deliver him, and honour him. With long life will I satisfy him, and shew him my salvation."

Yes, we honor our dead, but our Father honors His living sons and daughters by the provision of ongoing life and salvation. This is our rock to cling to, our prayer which acknowledges that they did not die in vain and that they have reaped the ultimate honor and reward. . . everlasting life.

Reuben's Song

It was years ago I first embarked
along embattled way,
and those who shared the sky with me
would laugh, would cry, would pray.

The bond of flying wing to wing
through flak-infested sky
was welded deep within our hearts --
a bond that would not die.

Ensuing years have not erased
our comradeship and care
for the precious cause of freedom
defended from the air.

But now the greatest of all flights
I've taken on my own --
and even as I climb on high,
I know I'm not alone.

I soar with angels skyward,
not needing man-made wings,
to discover deathless freedom
from mortal sense of things.

So wish me well, my brothers,
until we meet once more
in arm-to-arm formation
above life's golden shore.

Written in memory of a fellow B-24 pilot, May, 1988, and
initially published in "Ad Lib" (a publication of the 451st
World War II Bomb Group Association) and republished in
"B-17 Combat Crewmen & Wingmen".

God's Footsoldier

You walked the road through combat's hell
while praying this soon would end
for freedom's sake you gave your all,
side by side with closest friend.

But now you walk a higher path
with weapon laid aside;
you hold God's hand -- you feel His strength
and in His love abide.

March on brave soldier -- feel our love
as earth-ties fall away;
we set you free and yet we know
we'll meet again someday.

God's Ship-Call

You've sailed across horizon's span
toward shores we've yet to know;
our tear-washed faith sails with you now,
with love we let you go.

So now, brave sailor, feel the breeze
as angels steer the way;
know now the joy of freedom won;
discover endless day.

Wrath-vented seas of yesterday
give way to gentle calm;
The Captain of us all is here
to hold you in His palm.

Your Captain's Call

I've sailed rough seas before, dear ones,
and met and mastered foes,
etched in my heart, Soul-painted seas,
the calms between the blows.

But where I am today, my dears,
is not a storm-tossed sea;
lift up your hearts, and you will know
the Christ is here with me.

My love is with you, close at hand;
it whispers, "all is well;"
our Shepherd takes the helm today,
your sorrow to dispel.

Share my glad news with comrades close
and dear ones near and far,
I hold your hands -- I share your love,
beneath His guiding star.

Salute to a Fireman

You've faced terrible conflagrations,
fearlessly standing tall;
shown your concern in every way,
caretaker of us all.

But now you face a higher calling
in brightness of new day,
unselfishness reaping rich reward
without concern, dismay.

It's not easy now to let you go,
but love for you remains
to bolster spirit until that time
we drop our earthbound chains.

Above and Beyond

(Salute to a peace officer)

You've stepped through a door
that we all must face
at an age it would seem
much too young.
Your duty you handled
with steadfast resolve
"Badge of Courage"
your song to be sung.

We'll miss you, dear friend
and comrade in arms,
but we know you stand tall
in God's sight.
Heaven shines tonight
with a fresh new star
and our tears will reflect
its bright light.

So accept our salute
and fond farewell;
because of you
we stand in great pride.
"Above and beyond"
describes your brave act;
in our hearts
you remain at our side.

A revision of a poem commemorating a fallen officer.
Initially published in the newsletter of the San Diego Police
Officers Association.

Stand with Them

Strong they stood
in search of peace.
Support their prayers;
let warfare cease.

Section VIII

Remembering Our Pets

A pet is man's special friend
of its love, there is no end.

The Passing of Pets

Have you ever lost a much loved pet? In many households, a pet is considered to be a vital part of the family, perhaps the only family for some. A terrible sense of loss ensues unless we find an anchor of hope.

That anchor of hope and comfort rests in the understanding that all creatures are the offspring of a loving Creator and that only our limited mortal vision can seem to separate us from these very special family members. If a pet can be lost forever, separated from its Maker, then so can we. But Life's promise is greater than that.

The article that follows focuses on a single much adored pet in one household. She was a Golden Retriever named "Ginger-Snaps" ("Ginger" for short). Ginger was killed in a sudden, seemingly tragic, accident. The couple who adopted Ginger had no children, so this magnificent creature was treated as well or better than an only child.

Eventually Ginger was replaced with another beautiful dog, but she will always have a very special spot in the hearts of her family as well as her extended family.

Lessons Ginger Taught Us

Ginger has gone on her way now. The lesson for us to learn is that she is on her way, not lost forever. Can't you just see her leaping out over a beautiful blue lake or wagging her tail vigorously in anticipation of anyone who would pet her or throw a ball for her to retrieve?

All of the exquisite care and love you gave to Ginger would be meaningless if you and all who were privileged to know her had not learned some very important lessons while she was with us. Here are just a few of those lessons:

First of all, the length of time Ginger was with you was not nearly so important as the quality of your sharing. You grew by knowing and caring for her and she grew through a daily ministration of attention and care that few of us humans experience so fully. She is much richer today in all ways than when she came to you as a puppy. And that, in turn, enables her to give even more of herself now (and I know you think that is hardly possible) than she did when she was with you.

Second, Ginger taught us all a truer sense of family. Taken from her blood relatives at a very young age, she quickly overcame any sense of loss (as you must do now). And her demonstration of family expanded greatly -- not just your immediate family but other family members, friends, visitors, neighbors including her neighborhood animal friends, and on and on. There were no limits on her ability to enlarge her sense of family. And this is an important lesson for all of us. You cannot afford to accept any sense of a diminished family now. Ginger taught us all that family does not experience shrinkage. It only grows. The world cries out today for our demonstration of what constitutes true family. Ginger points the way.

Third, Ginger taught us what unswerving loyalty means. You could scold her, punish her, or even leave her for several days, but she never showed any sign of being resentful. You were her family. Nothing could take that great sense of belonging away from her. And today, she is finding new loyalties to her enlarged sense of family without for a moment sacrificing her love for you.

Fourth, Ginger gave the two of you the opportunity to rise above the mortal tendency of self-absorption. You could spend meaningful time sharing joy and buoyancy with her rather than trying to find more ways to make yourselves happier. Ginger teaches us that happiness is an inherent responsiveness, an ongoing activity rather than an illusive state of being to be sought after. Her joy was the product of love married to expectancy.

These are just a few lessons that we can learn from Ginger. I am sure that you two can think of many more. One thing is for sure. We are all the richer because Ginger came into our experience.

Charcoal's Love

How many evenings I spent
with my precious Charcoal in my lap or
close at hand.

As a kitten she seemed untiring
in her playfulness
but as we both matured
our love was communicated
in a silent acknowledgment
of our togetherness.

It has been so hard
to turn her loose,
but at long last I see her
in a different light. . .

I see a blending of the kitten
and the gentle, loving cat
bathed in the warmth of
her Father's tender care. . .

and like the promise of a rainbow
the urging of an angel voice
whispers, "I will never
deprive you of your
Charcoal's love
nor of Mine. . .

Know the nearness of that love,
cherish it, abide in it,
for it is the essence
of your very being
and of your Charcoal's too."

My Pet, My Friend

How special she was;
how special she is
for she will always
be a part of me.

We two were together
when my human friends
were too busy
to visit or call.

We were together
in the quiet moments;
in the enjoyment
of each other and
the world around us.

She has left me now
and yet. . .she really hasn't
for her loyalty and love
still permeate my home
and my heart.

In Conclusion. . .

Turning to Your Best Friend

Has "In the Dawn of a New Day" helped you? I hope so. If your life still seems empty, I suggest you search out and seek guidance from your best friend. You don't have to look far. In fact, you are your own best friend. Why? Because your spiritual selfhood is bursting at the seams to be expressed outwardly in new and exciting ways.

Most of us have talents that are never used or even suspected to be present. It may be one of the creative arts (music, writing, art, acting, etc.) or it may lie in our ability to share and care for our friends and fellow citizens. It seems to me that the best way we can pay tribute to our departed loved ones is by conducting a "treasure hunt" inside ourselves.

Age has nothing to do with this treasure hunt. If you found an actual buried treasure of gold and jewels, it would be more valuable today than when it was first buried, wouldn't it? To reach the treasure, you would have had to remove all of the dirt and other debris covering it. To reach the treasure of your "best friend", you have to remove grief, guilt, hurt, doubt, and self-depreciation which tend to hide your God-given talents and identity.

Simple acts touch hearts and give meaning to life. My heart was touched by the following example:

It was early morning in the park when I first saw the two. The woman pushing the wheel chair stopped in a level fenced area. Locking the wheels in place, and with utmost tenderness and care, she helped her lovely young charge to stand upright.

Assuring herself that her friend was standing firmly, the woman walked to the nearby fence. Plucking a small blossom, she returned to her trusting charge. Then, she carefully curled the seemingly useless fingers of one hand and placed the blossom there, encouraging the young woman to touch and examine the flower.

Each one of us can turn to our best friend for beautiful blossoms of creativity, loving-kindness, and self-forgetfulness, which will enrich the world and heal our searching hearts. The willingness to do so and the right motivation (the desire to bless our neighbors and loved ones) is all that is needed.

Remember, your talents, your resources are unique unto yourself. If you fail to use them the world is the poorer because of your withholding. Why not start your treasure hunt today?

About the Author

Sam Hornbeak was born in Wichita Falls, Texas, a few years after the conclusion of World War I, the second oldest of four children. His father, Sam, Sr., worked quite successfully in the oil industry until suffering some severe business reverses. His mother, Dorothy, worked as a seamstress and as a parachute-packer at Randolph Air Base during and after World War II. During most of his school days, Sam's family lived in San Antonio, Texas.

Times were not easy because of the great depression, but like so many families, the Hornbeaks learned to rely heavily on their church and its teachings for solutions. Sam describes the populace at that time as a "praying people", which accounted for his becoming a Bible student at a young age. He has continued that study and reliance upon God ever since.

Sam's paternal grandfather, born in East Texas, was a Presbyterian minister, a carpenter, and a founder and builder of churches. Ella Root Hornbeak, also a native Texan, was a petite and charming Irish lady, an ideal wife for an itinerant preacher.

His maternal grandfather, Millard Yeager, was from the East Coast, a teacher, county judge, and a graduate of the first law class of The University of Texas. Millard's wife, Alice Brown Yeager, was born in Palo Pinto County, Texas. Her father was a cowboy and rancher. Her grandfather was an itinerant preacher. After many years of invalidism and impending blindness, during which time many poems and articles she wrote were published in the leading Dallas newspaper, she returned to good health and was cured of the eye condition through her study of the Bible and related textbooks. She then spent many healthy years as a Christian Science practitioner. Her early writings reveal that she was an early women's rights advocate, fighting for suffrage and other rights for women. She encouraged Sam's writing during his school days, sending him a dollar for each poem he submitted to her (big bucks in the 30's)!

Sam became a combat bomber pilot in World War II, flying B-24's in the Italian Theater of Operations. He was awarded the Distinguished Flying Cross and the Air Medal with Clusters. Just as the old saying goes that there were not many atheists in foxholes, Sam never knew of any flying combat during the war. During these missions, when human life could be snuffed out at any moment, he turned strongly to God for comfort and the assurance of immortality. More than anything else, these wartime experiences strengthened his trust in a higher and more permanent sense of life.

During the Korean and Vietnam conflicts, Sam served part-time as a Christian Science Minister for the Armed Services in South Texas.

After the war, Sam graduated from The University of Texas with a BBA in accounting, subsequently spending many years in both the public and private sectors of accounting. Most of his writing during this time was in the form of business-related articles and newsletters, although a number of his poems and articles were published by his international church periodicals.

Now, in 1992, Sam has left the world of business and accounting to pursue full-time writing.

Quail Mountain Publishers
P. O. Box 773
Dewey, AZ 86327-0773

Telephone:
(602) 772-1540

Please write or call for the location of the nearest retail outlet where you may purchase this book. If the book cannot be found in your area, you may order directly from the publisher by mail.